The INSIDE GUIDE

WOMEN IN U.S. HISTORY

Women in the American Revolution

By Therese M. Shea

Cavendish Square

Published in 2025 by Cavendish Square Publishing, LLC
2544 Clinton Street Buffalo, NY 14224

First Edition

Library of Congress Cataloging-in-Publication Data

Names: Shea, Therese, author.
Title: Women in the American Revolution / Therese Shea.
Description: Buffalo : Cavendish Square Publishing, [2025] | Series: The inside guide: women in U.S. history | Includes index.
Identifiers: LCCN 2024024386 (print) | LCCN 2024024387 (ebook) | ISBN 9781502673060 (library binding) | ISBN 9781502673053 (paperback) | ISBN 9781502673077 (ebook)
Subjects: LCSH: United States–History–Revolution, 1775-1783–Women–Juvenile literature. | United States–History–Revolution, 1775-1783–Participation, Female–Juvenile literature.
Classification: LCC E276 .S54 2025 (print) | LCC E276 (ebook) | DDC 973.3/082–dc22
LC record available at https://lccn.loc.gov/2024024386
LC ebook record available at https://lccn.loc.gov/2024024387

Editor: Therese M. Shea
Copyeditor: Danielle Haynes
Designer: Deanna Lepovich

The photographs in this book are used by permission and through the courtesy of: Cover Shutterstock AI Generator/ Shutterstock.com; p. 4 Morphart Creation/Shutterstock.com; p. 5 PlainsOfAbraham2007/Wikimedia Commons; p. 6 Map of territorial growth 1775/Wikimedia Commons; p. 7 Pennsylvania Journal, Stamp Act announcement/Wikimedia Commons; p. 8 William Walcutt statue George III/Wikimedia Commons; p. 10 duncan1890/iStock.com; p. 12 Tory Refugees by Howard Pyle/Wikimedia Commons; p. 13 Spinninginthecolonialkitchen/Wikimedia Commons; p. 14 Everett Collection/Shutterstock.com; p. 15 Architect of the Capitol; p. 16 The Battle of Lexington/Wikimedia Commons; pp. 18, 20, 29 (left) courtesy of the Library of Congress; p. 19 Esther de Berdt Reed by Charles Peale/Wikimedia Commons; p. 21 Cowpens/Wikimedia Commons; p. 22 Leon Abdalian Collection/Boston Public Library; p. 24 Frontispiece and title page of The Female Review Life of Deborah Sampson, the Female Soldier in the War of Revolution/Wikimedia Commons; p. 25 NPG 86 168 Wright/Wikimedia Commons; p. 26 (left) Mrs James Warren (Mercy Otis), by John Singleton Copley/Wikimedia Commons; p. 26 (right) History of the Rise, Progress, and Termination of the American Revolution/ Wikimedia Commons; p. 27 Ludington statue 800/Wikimedia Commons; p. 29 (right) Keith Lance/iStock.com.

CPSIA compliance information: Batch #CWCSQ25: For further information contact Cavendish Square Publishing LLC at 1-877-980-4450.

Printed in the United States of America

CONTENTS

This illustration of Boston, Massachusetts, before the American Revolution shows colonists learning of new laws from Great Britain.

THE ROAD TO REVOLUTION

Chapter One

In the later half of the 1700s, the growing population of the 13 British colonies of North America became increasingly frustrated with British rule. For a long time before this, the colonies had largely been allowed to govern themselves. As long as the colonies remained loyal to Great Britain, they were allowed much freedom.

Then, Britain and France, along with each side's Native American **allies**, fought a costly war over North American territory from 1754 to 1763. British leaders wanted the colonists to help pay for this conflict. What followed

Through victory in the French and Indian War, Great Britain gained a great deal of territory in North America, including French-held lands east of the Mississippi River and Spanish-held Florida.

Fast Fact

Another reason for colonists' growing discontent with British rule was western territory. In the Proclamation of 1763, the British government set aside territory to the west of the colonies for Native Americans. However, some American colonists wanted the land for themselves.

was a period during which the British government tried to apply more control over its colonies, while American colonists largely resisted such efforts.

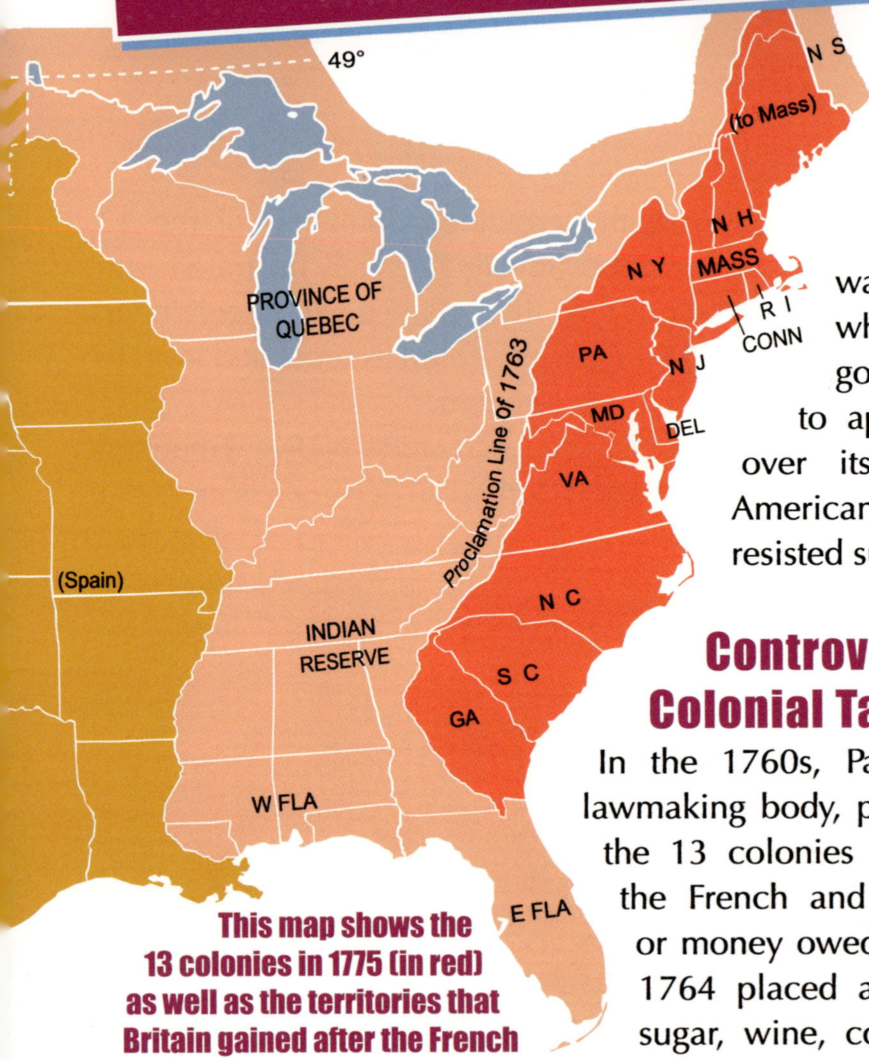

This map shows the 13 colonies in 1775 (in red) as well as the territories that Britain gained after the French and Indian War.

Controversial Colonial Taxes

In the 1760s, Parliament, Britain's lawmaking body, passed measures in the 13 colonies largely to pay for the French and Indian war debt, or money owed. The Sugar Act of 1764 placed a tax on imported sugar, wine, coffee, and **textiles**. The next year, the Stamp Act

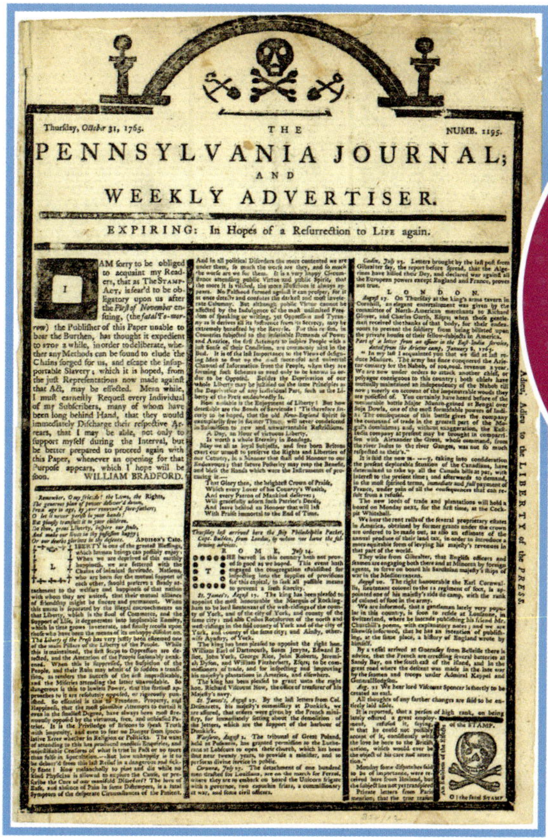
Thursday, October 31, 1765. THE NUMB. 1195.

PENNSYLVANIA JOURNAL; AND WEEKLY ADVERTISER.

EXPIRING: In Hopes of a Resurrection to LIFE again.

I AM sorry to be obliged to acquaint my Readers, that as The STAMP-ACT, is fear'd to be obligatory upon us after the First of November ensuing, (the fatal To-morrow) the Publisher of this Paper unable to bear the Burthen, has thought it expedient to STOP a while, in order to deliberate, whether any Methods can be found to elude the Chains forged for us, and escape the insupportable Slavery; which it is hoped, from the just Representations now made against that Act, may be effected. Mean while, I must earnestly Request every Individual of my Subscribers, many of whom have been long behind Hand, that they would immediately Discharge their respective Arrears, that I may be able, not only to support myself during the Interval, but be better prepared to proceed again with this Paper, whenever an opening for that Purpose appears, which I hope will be soon. WILLIAM BRADFORD.

A Pennsylvania paper condemns the Stamp Act in 1765. Newspapers were one of the paper products taxed by the measure.

Fast Fact

The Townshend Acts were a series of measures passed by Parliament in 1767. One of the acts taxed imported lead, tea, glass, paint, and paper, all items that the British thought colonists couldn't make themselves to avoid the taxes.

taxed paper items in the colonies. Previously, colonial governments—not Parliament—oversaw taxes on colonial goods. This taxation without representation (the colonies had no representatives in Parliament) greatly angered many colonists. Protests against the Stamp Act ended in its **repeal** in 1766. However, the same day of the repeal, Parliament announced its authority over the colonies in the Declaratory Act.

Patriots and Loyalists

People who rose up against British control called themselves patriots. Not all wanted independence from Great Britain. Some just wanted representation in Parliament. Others rejected the British government altogether. They thought it was time for the 13 colonies to govern

> **Fast Fact**
>
> Some families' loyalties were split. For example, Benjamin Franklin was a patriot, while his son William Franklin, royal governor of New Jersey, was a Loyalist.

themselves. More joined this group as the British ignored colonists' demands and even punished them for protesting.

Still, up to one-third of the colonial population considered themselves Loyalists, meaning they were loyal to Great Britain. A major reason was the economy. Some business owners were afraid of how protests or a war with Britain would affect their businesses. They thought accepting new taxes was the safest choice. Other colonists were Loyalists, also called Tories, because they worked for the British government. Taxes paid their salaries.

What Did Women Think?

Colonial women played meaningful roles, or parts, during this time, though their deeds often weren't recorded. While some women did speak out or act out as patriots, others remained Loyalists. In some cases, their opinions remain impossible to know because of a woman's place in colonial society. The government

Some Loyalists thought the patriots' protests were treason. Here, patriots tear down a statue of British king George III in New York City.

WHAT ABOUT THE NATIVE AMERICANS?

While white colonial women had some rights, women who were enslaved, Black, or Native American had even fewer under colonial law. When the American Revolution began, many Native American communities had to choose a side, though most wanted to stay out of the conflict. Native American women, many of whom held leadership roles in their own communities, likely had a say in this decision. Some Native nations, such as the Mohawk, chose the British side. Others, such as the Oneida, gave support to the colonists. After the British lost the war, they gave Native American lands to the west of the colonies to the Americans without consulting their Native allies.

didn't view women, especially married women, as individuals. Instead, they were "covered" by their husbands, who owned their money and property, or they were under the control of other male family members. Single women and widowed women had more rights, but still weren't viewed as equals to men. For the most part, women with Loyalist husbands were seen as Loyalists, and women in patriot families were thought to be patriots.

Women's experiences during this time differed greatly, depending on their wealth, race, education, and social class. However, women's actions overall were critical as the colonies began to fight for their independence—a fight which grew into the American Revolution.

The Liberty Tree in Boston was a meeting place for the Sons of Liberty, a secret organization that protested British rule of the American colonies.

THE DAUGHTERS OF LIBERTY

Chapter Two

Some protests of British laws and regulations were carefully planned by secret organizations. Perhaps the most famous protesters were the Sons of Liberty. The first group formed in 1765 in Boston in response to increasing colonial taxes. Other Sons of Liberty groups followed, but so too did an organization of patriot women called the Daughters of Liberty.

"With Ladies on Our Side"

The Daughters of Liberty formed in 1766 to organize protests against British taxation. Samuel Adams, a famous patriot and member of the Sons of Liberty, recognized the value of women taking part in the protests. He is reported to have said, "With ladies on our side, we can make every Tory tremble."

Fast Fact

Patriot women sometimes ostracized Loyalist women. Loyalist homes were robbed or damaged. Sometimes Loyalists had to flee from danger. Patriots in Loyalist communities experienced similar treatment.

One of the founders of the Daughters of Liberty, Sarah Bradlee Fulton, is sometimes called the "Mother of the Boston Tea Party" for her part in planning a famous

Patriots seized, or took, Loyalist property during the American Revolution. Loyalists leaving their home are shown here.

protest in 1773. As an answer to the British tax on tea, a group of colonists dressed as Native Americans and dumped 342 chests of tea into Boston Harbor. This protest **escalated** events that would lead to war.

Boycotts and Pledges

The Daughters of Liberty and other women's groups organized and supported **boycotts** of British imports. Near the end of the 1760s, many colonists who were against new taxes signed pledges, or promises, not to buy certain products. Merchants also pledged not to import certain products. The first such agreement was recorded in Boston, Massachusetts, in 1767. The pledge had more than 650 signatures; a number were women's names. Other areas had similar boycotts.

Women, as consumers of British goods such as fabric and tea, had to take part for the boycotts to work. This meant they had to make their own goods in some cases. Women organized what were called spinning bees or spinning matches to produce certain kinds of thread. After they had made thread from

Fast Fact

A 1769 *Boston Gazette* article reported that 45 women had gathered at a house to hold a spinning bee. By the day's end, they had created 602 **knots** of linen and 246 knots of cotton.

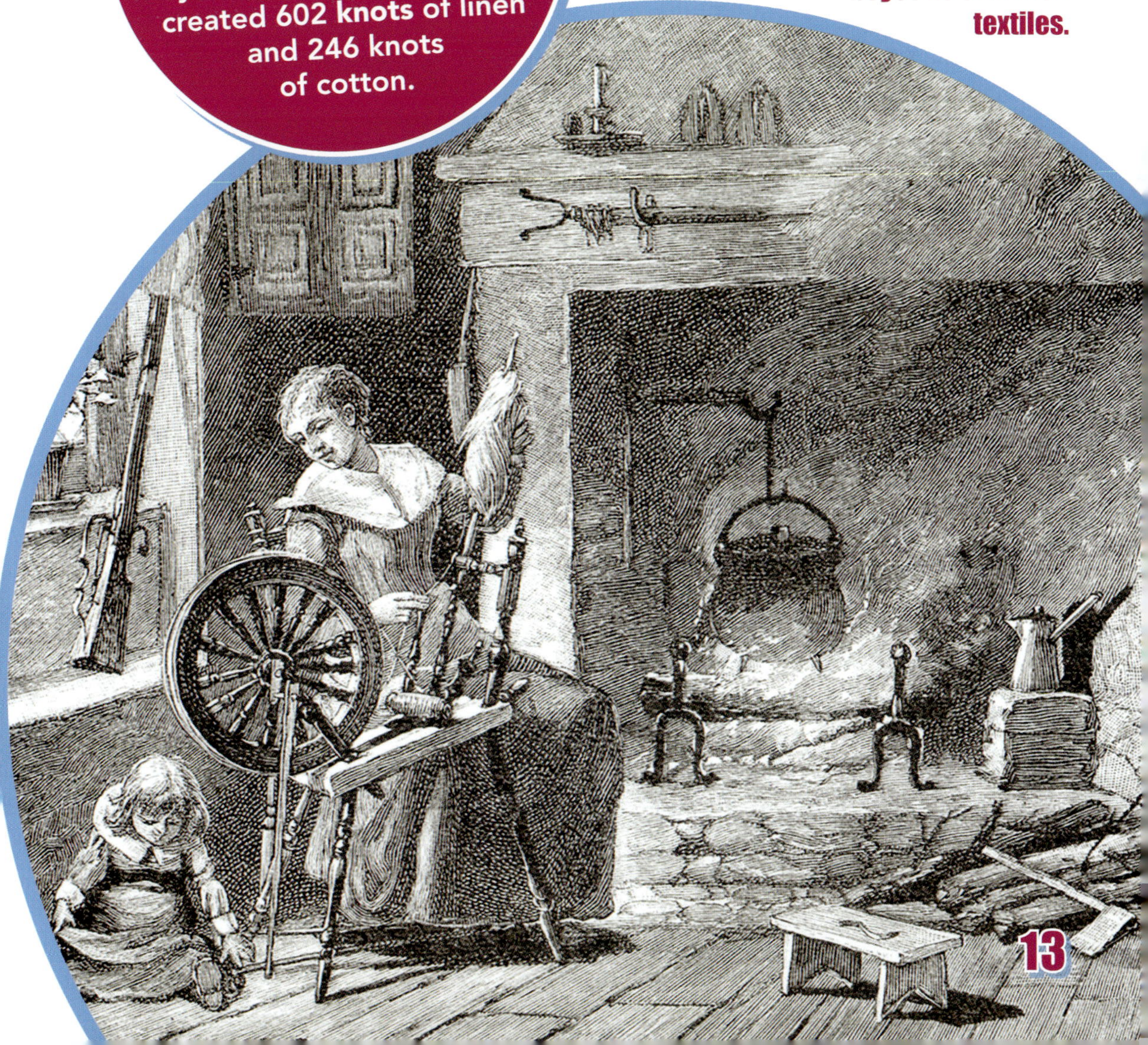

Many women had to learn how to make fabric for the first time during boycotts of British textiles.

FASHION FORWARD

Abigail Adams was the wife of patriot and future U.S. president John Adams. Her letters provide a valuable primary source for events around the American Revolution. In 1774, she wrote to British historian Catharine Sawbridge Macaulay about how women in Boston had replaced their fashionable British clothes with plain, colonial-made clothes: "For tho it was formerly the pride ... of Americans to indulge in the fashions and Manufactures of Great Brittain now [that] she threatens us with her chains we ... shall think ourselves more decently attired [clothed] in the coarse and plain vestures [clothing] of our own Manufactury."

Abigail Adams was an early supporter of women's rights. She famously asked her husband, John Adams, and other members of the Continental Congress in 1776 to "Remember the Ladies, and be more generous and favourable to them than your ancestors."

The First Continental Congress was a meeting of delegates, or representatives, from 12 of the 13 colonies. They met to make decisions together about the conflict with Britain.

Fast Fact

In December 1774, the First Continental Congress agreed to boycott all goods from Great Britain.

cotton or wool, they could use looms to weave fabrics. Textiles were the largest import to the colonies in the 1600s and 1700s, so a textile boycott was a major signal to Britain of the colonies' anger toward the textile tax.

The fabrics made in the colonies, sometimes called homespun fabrics, were often not as well-made or fashionable as those from Britain. However, wearing homemade clothes became a sign of the patriot spirit. Because women were mainly the ones who made the clothing, they were a key part of this protest.

Historical records report colonial women in Massachusetts encouraged their husbands and sons to fight at the Battles of Lexington and Concord, the first battles of the American Revolution.

Chapter Three

THE WAR BEGINS

With the British government and colonial leadership unable to agree on colonial governance, the American Revolution began with the Battles of Lexington and Concord on April 19, 1775. The Second Continental Congress issued the Declaration of Independence in 1776, establishing the United States. Women continued to be a support to the American cause during the war. Many remained at home to run family businesses and farms. Others followed their husbands from battlefield to battlefield.

Camp Followers

Women played an invaluable and often unrecorded part in the **Continental Army**. Those who accompanied the soldiers as they traveled throughout the country were called camp followers. Thousands of women and children followed the British and American forces.

Fast Fact

Free Black women could follow the Continental Army only if their husbands were soldiers or if soldiers employed them. Some soldiers forced their enslaved workers to follow the army.

Fast Fact

Margaret Corbin was another camp follower who may have been a source of the Molly Pitcher story. She took her husband's place at a cannon at the Battle of Fort Washington in 1776. She was captured by the British but later released.

Some camp followers were wives and children of soldiers. Some had nowhere else to go, as their homes had been destroyed by the fighting. Many women performed necessary duties for the army, such as preparing food and cleaning uniforms and sheets, which kept soldiers healthy. Many female camp followers were nurses. The number of sick and wounded soldiers was sometimes too high for the doctors and other medical staff in the army ranks to care for, so nurses were necessary.

Some camp followers ended up in battle. This was the case in the story of Molly Pitcher, a somewhat legendary figure who was based on

Mary Ludwig Hays, who may have inspired the legend of Molly Pitcher, later received a pension for her heroic deeds at the Battle of Monmouth.

real women who performed similar feats. Molly may have been Mary Ludwig Hays, a woman who followed her husband, William Hays, a soldier in the Continental Army. When William was wounded at the Battle of Monmouth in 1778, Mary took his place at a cannon.

Raising Funds for the Army

In 1780, a woman's organization launched in Philadelphia, Pennsylvania, to help fund the Continental Army. Esther de Berdt Reed was one of the founders of the Ladies' Association of Philadelphia. She appealed to women to give up buying luxuries and donate money to the army instead.

The Ladies' Association raised a substantial amount. They used the money to buy fabric. Members made over 2,000 shirts for Continental soldiers, sewing their own names into the clothing as a reminder of women's contributions to the cause of independence. Esther Reed died less than a year after co-founding the Ladies' Association, but her work became well

For her efforts with the Ladies' Association of Philadelphia, Esther de Berdt Reed was named a member of the Daughters of Liberty.

known and inspired similar organizations in other states.

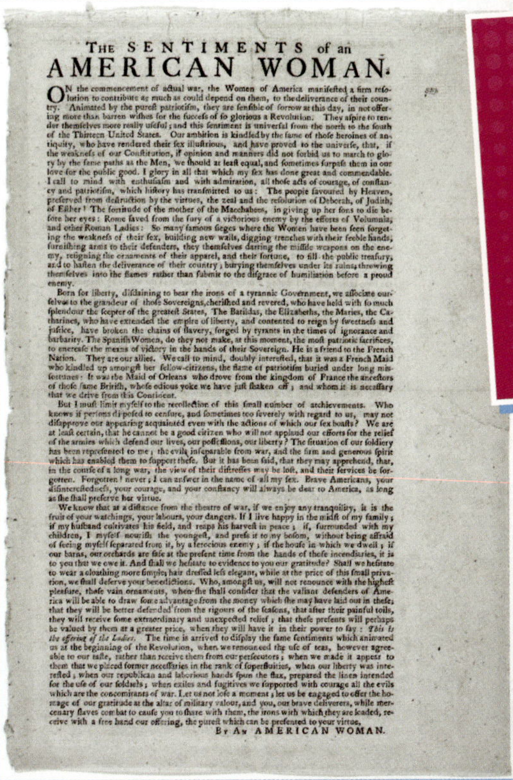

THE SENTIMENTS of an AMERICAN WOMAN.

ON the commencement of actual war, the Women of America manifeſted a firm reſolution to contribute as much as could depend on them, to the deliverance of their country. Animated by the pureſt patriotiſm, they are ſenſible of ſorrow at this day, in not offering more than barren wiſhes for the ſucceſs of ſo glorious a Revolution. They aſpire to render themſelves more really uſeful; and this ſentiment is univerſal from the north to the ſouth of the Thirteen United States. Our ambition is kindled by the fame of thoſe heroines of antiquity, who have rendered their ſex illuſtrious, and have proved to the univerſe, that, if the weakneſs of our Conſtitution, if opinion and manners did not forbid us to march to glory by the ſame paths as the Men, we ſhould at leaſt equal, and ſometimes ſurpaſs them in our love for the public good. I glory in all that which my ſex has done great and commendable. I call to mind with enthuſiaſm and with admiration, all thoſe acts of courage, of conſtancy and patriotiſm, which hiſtory has tranſmitted to us: The people favoured by Heaven, preſerved from deſtruction by the virtues, the zeal and the reſolution of Deborah, of Judith, of Eſther! The fortitude of the mother of the Macchabees, in giving up her ſons to die before her eyes: Rome ſaved from the fury of a victorious enemy by the efforts of Volumnia, and other Roman Ladies: So many famous ſieges where the Women have been ſeen forgeting the weakneſs of their ſex, building new walls, digging trenches with their feeble hands, furniſhing arms to their defenders, they themſelves darting the miſſile weapons on the enemy, reſigning the ornaments of their apparel, and their fortune, to fill the public treaſury, and to haſten the deliverance of their country; burying themſelves under its ruins; throwing themſelves into the flames rather than ſubmit to the diſgrace of humiliation before a proud enemy.

Born for liberty, diſdaining to bear the irons of a tyrannic Government, we aſſociate ourſelves to the grandeur of thoſe Sovereigns, cheriſhed and revered, who have held with ſo much ſplendour the ſcepter of the greateſt States, The Batildas, the Elizabeths, the Maries, the Catharines, who have extended the empire of liberty, and contented to reign by ſweetneſs and juſtice, have broken the chains of ſlavery, forged by tyrants in the times of ignorance and barbarity. The Spaniſh Women, do they not make, at this moment, the moſt patriotic ſacrifices, to encreaſe the means of victory in the hands of their Sovereign. He is a friend to the French Nation. They are our allies. We call to mind, doubly intereſted, that it was a French Maid who kindled up amongſt her fellow-citizens, the flame of patriotiſm buried under long misfortunes: It was the Maid of Orleans who drove from the kingdom of France the anceſtors of thoſe ſame Britiſh, whoſe odious yoke we have juſt ſhaken off; and whom it is neceſſary that we drive from this Continent.

But I muſt limit myſelf to the recollection of this ſmall number of atchievements. Who knows if perſons diſpoſed to cenſure, and ſometimes too ſeverely with regard to us, may not diſapprove our appearing acquainted even with the actions of which our ſex boaſts? We are at leaſt certain, that he cannot be a good citizen who will not applaud our efforts for the relief of the armies which defend our lives, our poſſeſſions, our liberty? The ſituation of our ſoldiery has been repreſented to me; the evils inſeparable from war, and the firm and generous ſpirit which has enabled them to ſupport theſe. But it has been ſaid, that they may apprehend, that, in the courſe of a long war, the view of their diſtreſſes may be loſt, and their ſervices be forgotten. Forgotten! never; I can anſwer in the name of all my ſex. Brave Americans, your diſintereſtedneſs, your courage, and your conſtancy will always be dear to America, as long as ſhe ſhall preſerve her virtue.

We know that at a diſtance from the theatre of war, if we enjoy any tranquility, it is the fruit of your watchings, your labours, your dangers. If I live happy in the midſt of my family; if my huſband cultivates his field, and reaps his harveſt in peace; if, ſurrounded with my children, I myſelf nouriſh the youngeſt, and preſs it to my boſom, without being affraid of ſeeing myſelf ſeparated from it, by a ferocious enemy; if the houſe in which we dwell; if our barns, our orchards are ſafe at the preſent time from the hands of thoſe incendiaries, it is to you that we owe it. And ſhall we heſitate to evidence to you our gratitude? Shall we heſitate to wear a cloathing more ſimple; hair dreſſed leſs elegant, while at the price of this ſmall privation, we ſhall deſerve your benedictions. Who, amongſt us, will not renounce with the higheſt pleaſure, thoſe vain ornaments, when ſhe ſhall conſider that the valiant defenders of America will be able to draw ſome advantage from the money which ſhe may have laid out in theſe; that they will be better defended from the rigours of the ſeaſons, that after their painful toils, they will receive ſome extraordinary and unexpected relief; that theſe preſents will perhaps be valued by them at a greater price, when they will have it in their power to ſay: *This is the offering of the Ladies.* The time is arrived to diſplay the ſame ſentiments which animated us at the beginning of the Revolution, when we renounced the uſe of teas, however agreeable to our taſte, rather than receive them from our perſecutors; when we made it appear to them that we placed former neceſſaries in the rank of ſuperfluities, when our liberty was intereſted; when our republican and laborious hands ſpun the flax, prepared the linen intended for the uſe of our ſoldiers; when exiles and fugitives we ſupported with courage all the evils which are the concomitants of war. Let us not loſe a moment; let us be engaged to offer the homage of our gratitude at the altar of military valour, and you, our brave deliverers, while mercenary ſlaves combat to cauſe you to ſhare with them, the irons with which they are loaded, receive with a free hand our offering, the pureſt which can be preſented to your virtue.

BY AN AMERICAN WOMAN.

The broadside titled "Sentiments of an American Woman" said: "If opinion and manners did not forbid us [women] to march to glory by the same paths as the Men, we should at least equal, and sometimes surpass [exceed] them in our love for the public good."

Fast Fact

The Ladies' Association of Philadelphia began with the publication of a broadside titled "Sentiments of an American Woman." The author maintained that women were as much patriots as men.

Working From Home

Part of the success of the Daughters of Liberty, the Ladies' Association of Philadelphia, and similar groups was that they operated within women's normal lives. Colonial women were most often at home, taking care of their family and household. As patriot women took part in revolutionary activities, they most ofen did these at home or within their social circles, so there was little pushback from colonial society. Newspapers from that time praised women for caring for both family and country through the end of the war in 1783 and beyond.

SEEKING FREEDOM

In November 1775, John Murray, the Earl of Dunmore and royal governor of Virginia, persuaded some Americans to join the Loyalists. Dunmore's Proclamation promised freedom to **indentured servants** and enslaved people who left their patriot enslavers to fight against American forces. In 1779, Henry Clinton, commander of the British North American forces, granted freedom to all people enslaved by patriots. Enslaved people, if able to escape, had to make a choice. Thousands sided with the British, hoping for eventual freedom—including an enslaved teenage girl from George Washington's Virginia farm. Many of these freedom-seekers worked as servants for the British army at first.

Many formerly enslaved people found freedom by following the British. The British transported them to Canada, the Caribbean, or Britain. Others were later enslaved again. Thousands of Black patriots fought with the Continental Army as well. One such patriot is depicted in this painting of the Battle of Cowpens.

Many colonial women's lives were in danger during the American Revolution. Deborah Sampson was famously injured while pretending to be a man so she could serve in the army.

SOLDIERS, SPIES, AND MUCH MORE

Chapter Four

Some women left behind their duties as wife, mother, and homemaker during the American Revolution. Although women weren't officially allowed to fight in the Continental Army, a few found a way. The most famous example was Deborah Sampson.

A Continental Soldier

In 1782, Sampson joined the 4th Massachusetts Regiment of the Continental Army disguised as a man. She called herself by her dead brother's name, Robert Shurtleff. That same year, she was wounded in the head and leg during a battle in New York. Fearful that doctors would find out she was a woman, she left the hospital and removed a bullet from her own leg with a knife.

> **Fast Fact**
>
> Deborah Sampson tried to join the army once before 1782 but the military rejected her when they discovered she was a woman.

An army doctor found out Sampson was a woman—and not a male soldier—when she fell ill with a fever in 1783, but he kept her identity a secret. After her service was done, Sampson went on to marry and have a

Deborah Sampson was named the official heroine of Massachusetts in 1983.

family. She later gave talks about her wartime service, sometimes dressing as a soldier.

Spies

Some colonial women could actually say they altered the course of the war. As spies, they collected important information the military used in its planning. They were often not suspected of spying because they were women.

Anna Strong lived on Long Island in New York. She was part of a spy group called the Culper Ring. When Strong had information, she hid it in a location and signaled another spy to collect it by arranging clothing a certain way on a clothesline.

Fast Fact

Patriot and Sons of Liberty member Paul Revere helped Sampson receive an army pension.

Patience Lovell Wright was an American artist living in London, England, where she heard British plans for the war from leaders in Parliament and in the king's court. She is said to have

Patience Wright was a sculptor of wax figures who was famous in the American colonies and Great Britain.

hidden messages in statues she made and sent them to Benjamin Franklin and Thomas Jefferson.

Lydia Darragh had her Philadelphia home taken over by British troops in 1777. Hiding in a closet, she listened to soldiers' plans to surprise Continental troops. She passed that information to patriots.

Women's Work

Women's roles in the American Revolution were many: protesters, boycotters, spinners, weavers, clothing makers, nurses, cooks, fundraisers, soldiers, and spies. Most were ordinary women who also took care of families, households, and businesses.

HISTORIAN OF THE REVOLUTION: MERCY OTIS WARREN

During a time when women were expected to be silent on politics, Mercy Otis Warren spoke out. Mercy and her husband, James Warren, a Massachusetts lawmaker, were early patriots. They hosted meetings in their home to talk about British policies. James encouraged Mercy, who had largely conducted her own education, to write. She published political dramas that featured her opinions and were attacks on the British government. She supported protests and encouraged other women to do the same. Mercy Otis Warren was also one of the earliest historians of the events of the American Revolution, publishing *History of the Rise, Progress and Termination of the American Revolution* in 1805.

Mercy Otis Warren hoped the new government of the United States would provide more democratic opportunities for women.

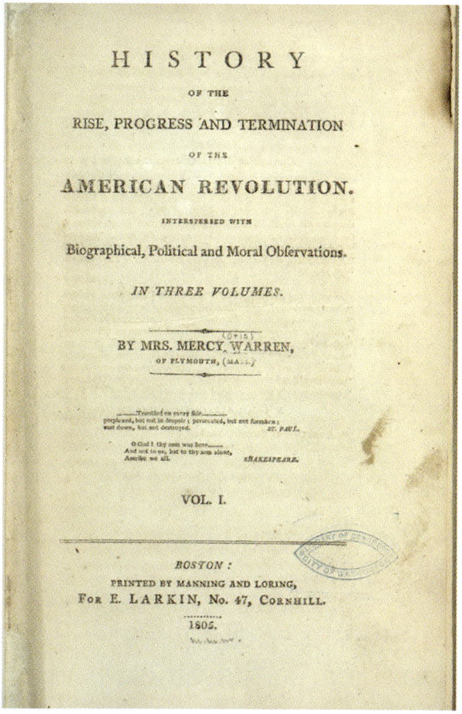

HISTORY

OF THE

RISE, PROGRESS AND TERMINATION

OF THE

AMERICAN REVOLUTION.

INTERSPERSED WITH

Biographical, Political and Moral Obfervations.

IN THREE VOLUMES.

BY MRS. MERCY (OTIS) WARREN,

OF PLYMOUTH, (MASS.)

——Troubled on every side——
perplexed, but not in despair; persecuted, but not forsaken;
cast down, but not destroyed. *ST. PAUL.*

O God! thy arm was here——
And not to us, but to thy arm alone,
Ascribe we all. *SHAKESPEARE.*

VOL. I.

BOSTON:

PRINTED BY MANNING AND LORING,

FOR E. LARKIN, No. 47, CORNHILL.

1805.

On April 26, 1777, 16-year-old Sybil Ludington of New York rode her horse to alert people in nearby communities that the British were planning an attack nearby.

Many took part in the war because they believed in the patriot cause. Some, like Abigail Adams, hoped the future United States would allow women to participate in government. However, it would be many years before American women were truly included in the new **democracy**.

The names of many female heroes of the American Revolution have likely been lost to time, but no true history should leave out women's part in helping the patriots win the war.

Fast Fact

Polly Cooper, a Native American woman, traveled more than 400 miles (644 kilometers) with other Oneida in 1778 to deliver corn to starving Continental troops at Valley Forge, Pennsylvania. She stayed to help the soldiers.

A TIMELINE OF WOMEN OF THE AMERICAN REVOLUTION

1766
The Daughters of Liberty organize protests of British taxation.

1767
Women in Boston pledge to boycott British goods. Women begin to participate in spinning bees to create homespun fabric.

1772
Mercy Otis Warren writes a story called "The Adulator" that criticizes the British governor of Massachusetts's policies.

1773
The Boston Tea Party protest takes place, partly planned by Daughters of Liberty member Sarah Bradlee Fulton.

1775
On April 19, the Battles of Lexington and Concord begin the American Revolution. Patriot women encourage male family members to fight. "Camp followers" begin to care for the soldiers.

1776
Abigail Adams encourages her husband to "Remember the Ladies" as the Continental Congress works to establish an independent nation.

1777
On December 2, Lydia Darragh overhears British military information and helps save George Washington's troops from a surprise attack.

1778
Polly Cooper, an Oneida woman, delivers corn to starving Continental troops at Valley Forge, Pennsylvania. On June 28, Mary Ludwig Hayes takes her husband's place at a cannon during the Battle of Monmouth.

1780
Esther de Berdt Reed helps establish the Ladies' Association of Philadelphia to raise funds for the Continental Army.

1782
Deborah Sampson joins the Continental Army disguised as a man. She serves until the end of the war in 1783.

THINK ABOUT IT!

1. Why do you think it was easier for wealthy white women to support the patriot cause than colonial women of other backgrounds?
2. What do you think might have happened to soldiers without camp followers?
3. Why do you think the story of Molly Pitcher became linked to several stories of women in the American Revolution?
4. Which woman in this book would you like to learn more about? Why?

GLOSSARY

ally: One of two or more people or groups who work together.

boycott: The act of refusing to have dealings with a person or business in order to force change.

broadside: A large sheet of paper with printing on one side.

Continental Army: The army of American colonists during the American Revolution, led by General George Washington.

democracy: A form of government based on the free and equal right of every person to participate in their government.

escalate: To make worse or more serious.

indentured servant: One who signs a contract agreeing to be bound to work for another for a set period of time in exchange for specific benefits.

knot: A length of thread or yarn coiled up and tied up into a unit called a skein or hank.

ostracize: To not let someone be a part of a group on purpose.

pension: Money that a company or the government pays to someone who is old or sick and no longer works.

repeal: To do away with.

textile: Cloth or fabric that is made by weaving thread together.

treason: The crime of attempting to bring down your country's government or of aiding your country's enemies during war.

FIND OUT MORE

Books

Connors, Kathleen. *Forgotten Facts About Life During the American Revolution*. Buffalo, NY: Enslow Publishing, 2024.

Gunderson, Jessica. *Sybil Ludington Rides to the Rescue: Courageous Kid of the American Revolution*. North Mankato, MN: Capstone Press, 2021.

Lowe, Mifflin. *Forgotten Founders: Black Patriots, Women Soldiers, and Other Thinkers and Heroes Who Shaped Early America.* Fresno, CA: Bushel & Peck Books, 2022.

Websites

Britannica Kids: American Revolution
kids.britannica.com/kids/article/American-Revolution/353711
Read more about the background, battles, and outcomes of the war.

Museum of the American Revolution: A Woman's War
www.amrevmuseum.org/big-idea-4-a-womens-war
Find out more about how women of different backgrounds experienced the war.

World History Encyclopedia: Women in the American Revolution
www.worldhistory.org/article/2453/women-in-the-american-revolution/
Learn more about this fascinating subject from the World History Encyclopedia.

Publisher's note to educators and parents: Our editors have carefully reviewed these websites to ensure that they are suitable for students. Many websites change frequently, however, and we cannot guarantee that a site's future contents will continue to meet our high standards of quality and educational value. Be advised that students should be closely supervised whenever they access the internet.

INDEX